Roger Hudson
Solo Guitar Works Volume 3, 2007-2020

Standard Notation Only Version

©2021 Roger Hudson ©2021 Roger Hudson Music
ALL RIGHTS RESERVED, INTERNATIONAL COPYRIGHT SECURED, ASCAP

No part of this publication may be reproduced in whole or in part, or stored in a retrieval system, or transmitted in any form or by any means, electronic, mechanical, photocopy, or otherwise, without written permission of the author/publisher

Cover Art by Elijah Hudson
Back cover photo by Dimitri Jansen
www.rogerhudson.com

Preface and Timeline

As was the case with _Roger Hudson Solo Guitar Works Volumes 1 and 2_, this collection is a reflection of yet another transitional period. The solo pieces in this collection come from my latter years in Nashville up to my present life (since 2011) in Florida. Some of the pieces in this group – "Moon Tide", "Floating Dream", "Waiting for a Friend" - are reminiscent of my earlier neo-impressionist tendencies. Other, more recent works represent a departure into lesser known territory. Some selections – including the three mentioned above – first appeared in _The Roger Hudson Guitar Method_ as early repertoire pieces for students. Other works, including many new ones, are intended for the technique and artistic maturity of an advanced guitarist.

This collection begins at a time when I was reaching some milestones in life. By 2007, I had been putting together a Nashville-based musical career consisting of teaching, composing, music journalism, recording and performing. Several solos from my 2009 _Delta_ CD are included in this book: "Almeria High Noon" (solo version)," BluesRay", "Sailing for America", and "Seven Heaven". The Delta CD is my latest album release. Although I do plan on releasing more "albums" in the future, it is the case that this _Roger Hudson Guitar Works Volume 3_ contains mostly music that has not been recorded as part of a traditional record release. For listening purposes, many "unreleased" titles included here can be found on YouTube's _Roger Hudson Channel._

After the _Delta_ CD, I began to feel some wanderlust…and age 50 pressing in on me! In 2010 the idea of being an old guitar player in Nashville didn't particularly appeal to me. The music business was changing. Even "A-Team" session musicians weren't getting as many calls for work. The two colleges where I had been teaching for years periodically murmured that they might someday make me a full-time instructor. What probably needed to happen was for me to go into a doctoral program to even be considered. My plan was that I was not going to be enrolling in a doctoral program. So, it was in 2011, with the help of my friend Jimmy Moore, that I took a guitar instructor job in Florida at Manatee School for the Arts. Thankfully, after seeing the beautiful beaches and imagining coat-less winters, my family were up for the move.

My 14 years living in Nashville were enjoyable ones. I learned what I wanted to do and what I didn't want to do. I made lifelong friendships with some amazingly talented people. The biggest lesson that I learned was that I loved composing music more than anything! With that in mind, it does not really matter so much where I live. The Florida move was an inspiration artistically and freed me up to concentrate on composing and publishing. Alas, here we are!

Finally, the year 2020 was a strange one. Due to the global COVID-19 pandemic and complicated life which ensued, I characterize 2020 as _surreal_. Included in this collection are _"Five Surrealities for Solo Guitar"_ and _"Departure: 2020"._ These works represent some of my musical impressions of 2020.

As was the case in Volumes 1 and 2, I did make updates (and corrections) to earlier versions of some compositions.

Roger Hudson - January 2021

Roger Hudson
Solo Guitar Works Volume 3
2007-2020

Table of Contents

4 -	Almeria High Noon
8 -	BluesRay
10 -	Celebration and Reflection
14 -	Daydream
16 -	Departure: 2020
18 -	Floating Dream
19 -	Ghost Mariner's Waltz
22 -	Got Rhythm?
23 -	January
27 -	Kelly's Green Jig
28 -	Labyrinth
30 -	Memphis Mambo
34 -	Midnight Flight
40 -	Mixed Emotions
41 -	Moon Tide
42 -	Old Florida
45 -	Sailing for America
46 -	Scarborough Jazz Fair
50 -	Seven Heaven
51 -	Seventies Chick
54 -	Shadows of Capoeira
56 -	Surreality 1
59 -	Surreality 2
62 -	Surreality 3
65 -	Surreality 4
68 -	Surreality 5
73 -	Sweet Surprise
74 -	Um Puoco de Bossa
75 -	Waiting for a Friend

©2021 Roger Hudson Music
All Rights Reserved. International copyright reserved. ASCAP
www.rogerhudson.com

Almería High Noon
Solo Guitar Version

Roger Hudson

©2007 Roger Hudson ©2020 Roger Hudson Music. All Rights Reserved. International Copyright Secured. ASCAP

BluesRay

Roger Hudson

Intentional blank page to minimize page turns

Celebration and Reflection
for Byron Fogo's 70th Birthday

Roger Hudson

Daydream

Roger Hudson

Intentional blank page to minimize page turns

Departure: 2020

Roger Hudson

Floating Dream

Roger Hudson

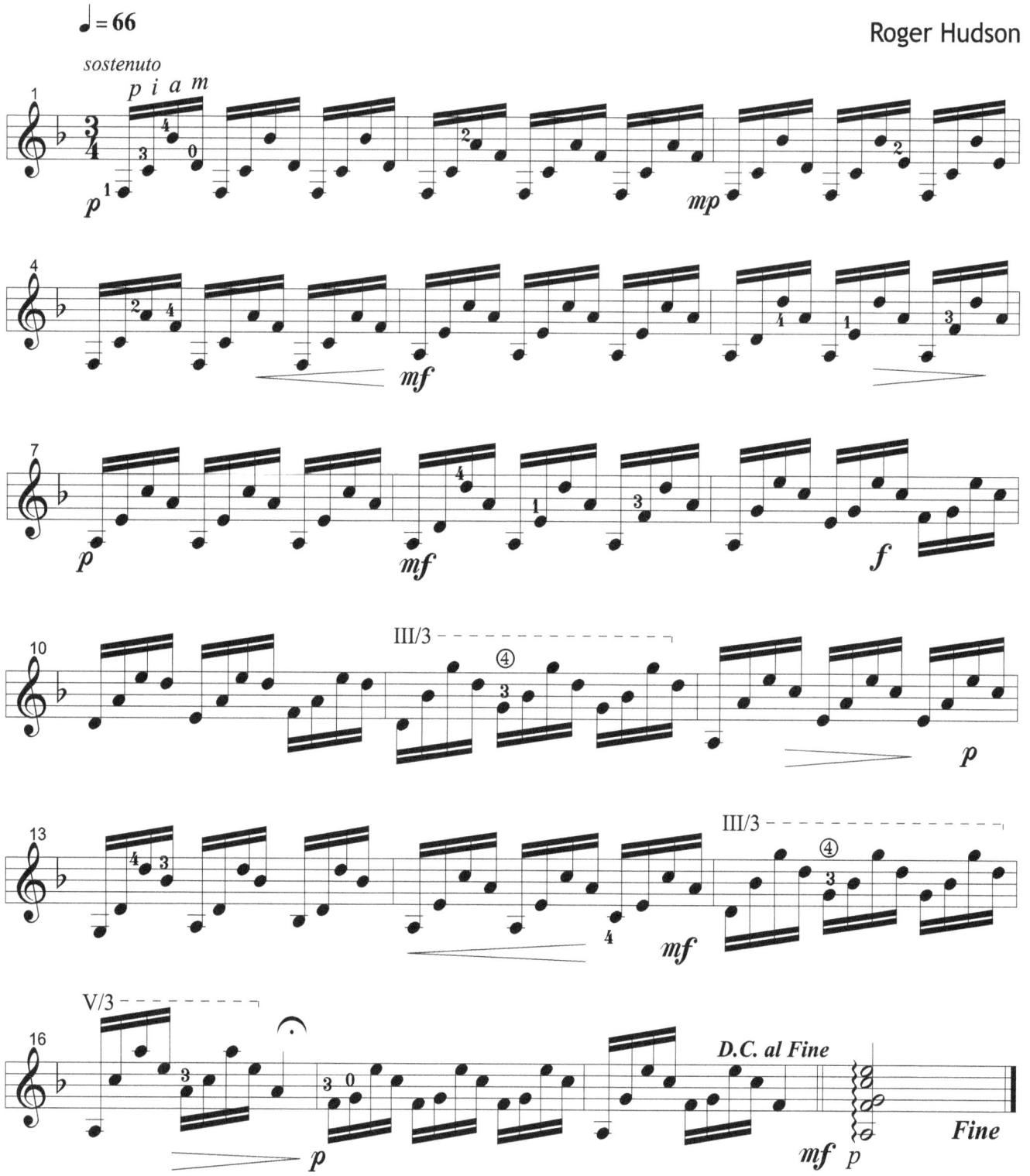

Ghost Mariner's Waltz

Roger Hudson

Got Rhythm?

Roger Hudson

January

for Dr. Erol Ozsever

Roger Hudson

⑥ = D

Slowly and Spaciously

Intentional blank page to minimize page turns

Kelly's Green Jig

Roger Hudson

Labyrinth

Roger Hudson

Memphis Mambo

Roger Hudson

Intentional blank page to minimize page turns

Midnight Flight

Roger Hudson

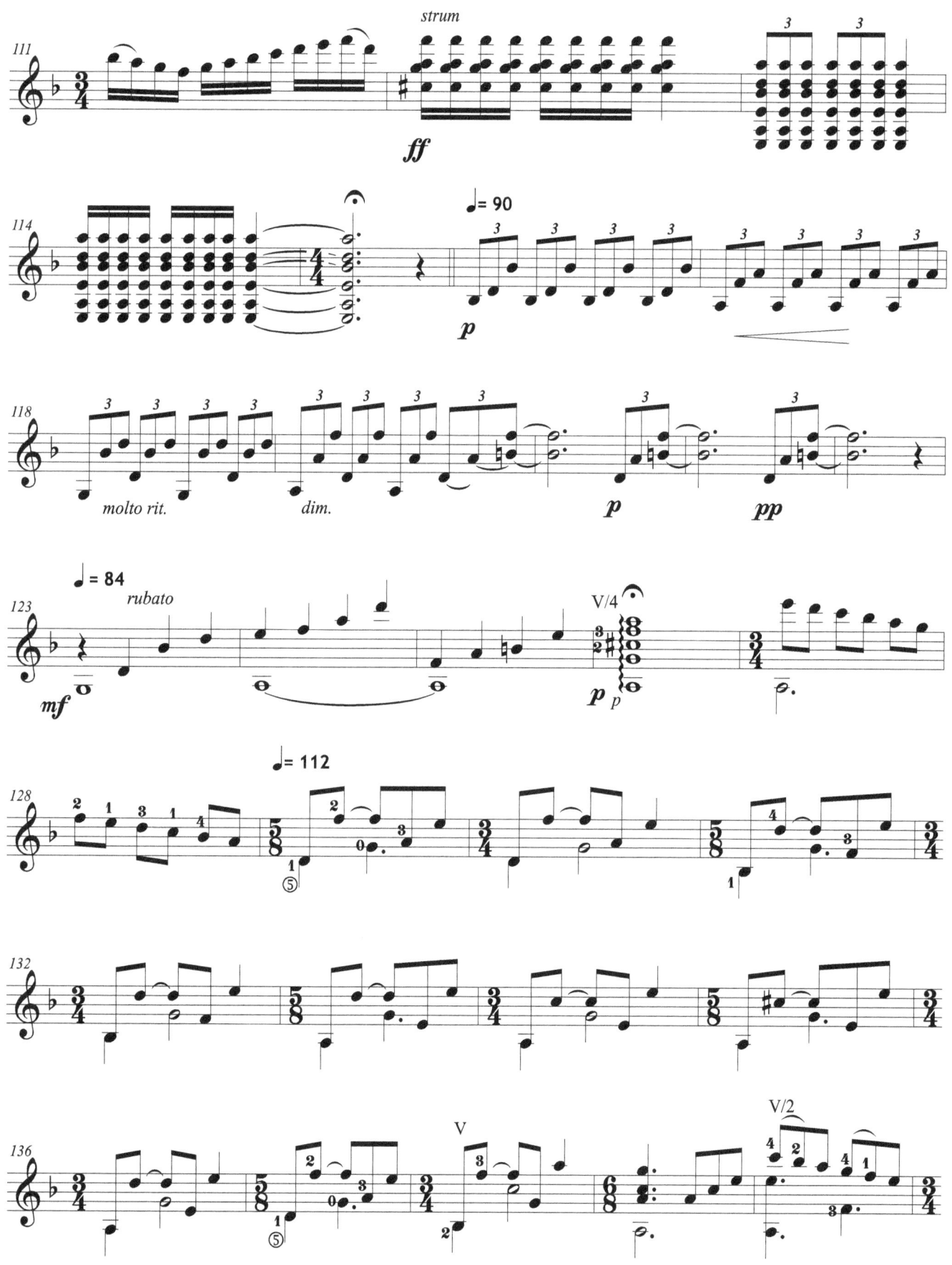

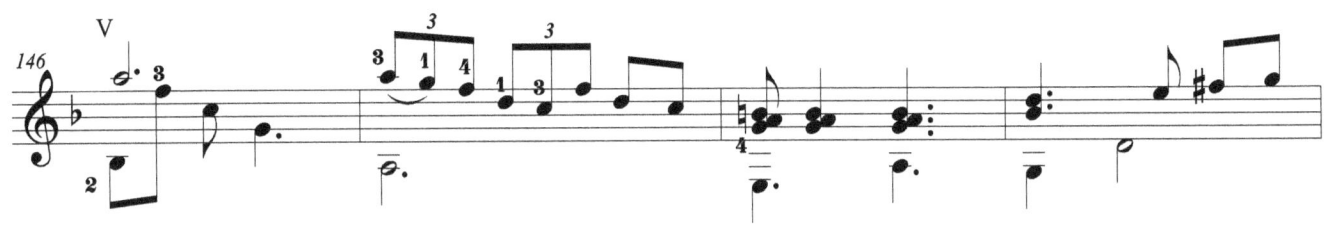

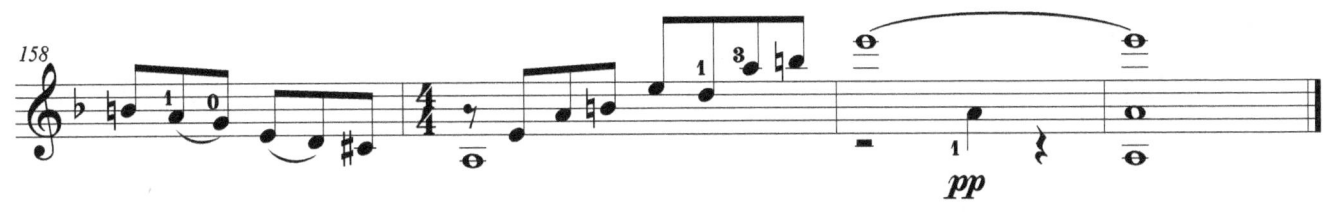

Mixed Emotions

Roger Hudson

Moon Tide

Roger Hudson

Old Florida

for Dr. Jimmy Moore

Roger Hudson

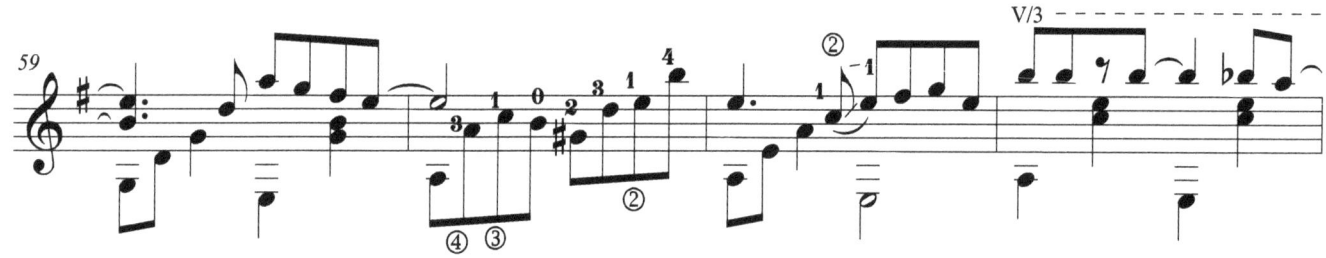

Sailing for America

Roger Hudson

©2007 Roger Hudson © 2020 Roger Hudson Music. All Rights Reserved. International Copyright Secured. ASCAP

Scarborough Jazz Fair

Roger Hudson
Traditional English Folksong

©2016 Roger Hudson ©2020 Roger Hudson Music. All Rights Reserved. International Copyright Secured. ASCAP

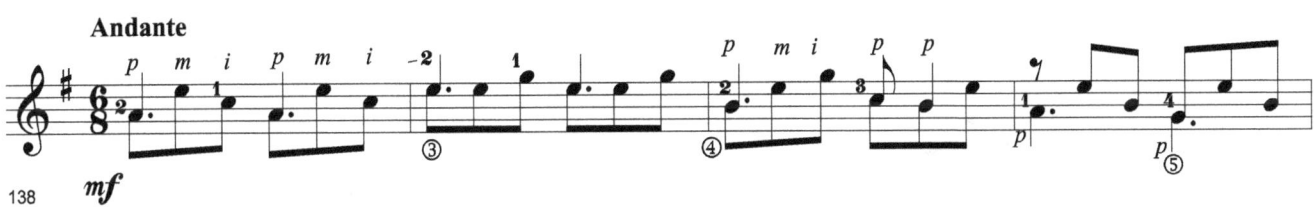
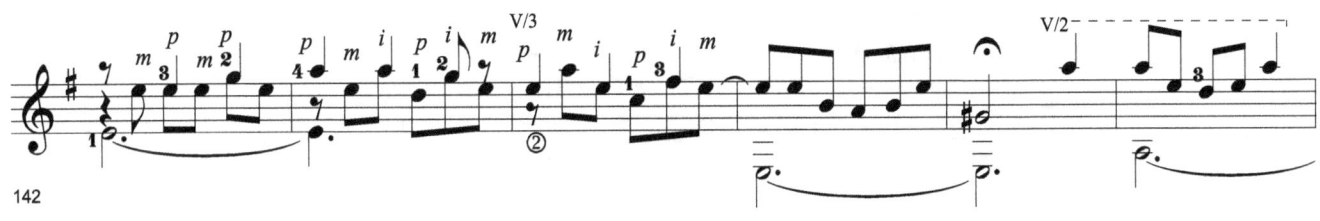

49

Seven Heaven

Roger Hudson

Seventies Chick

Roger Hudson

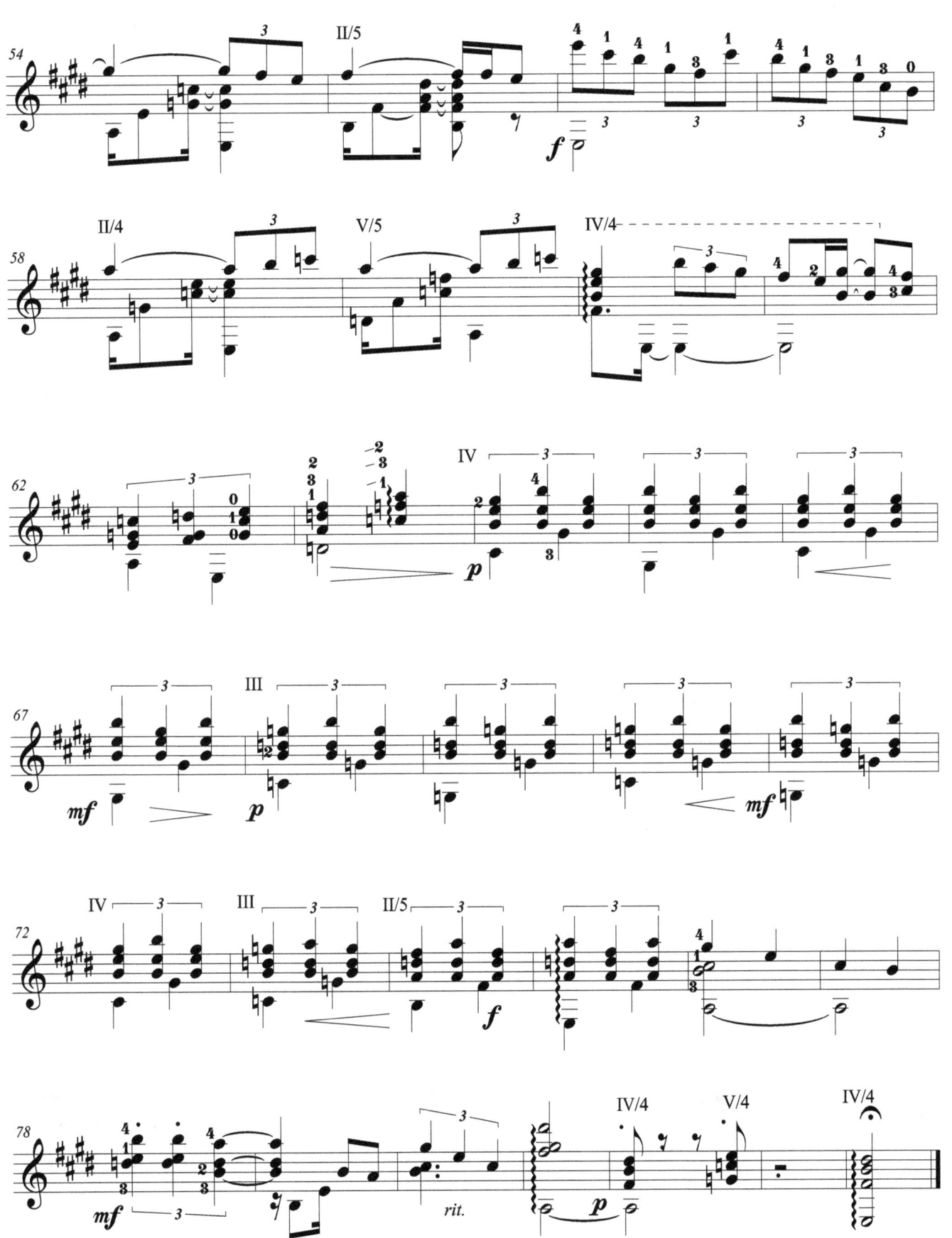

Shadows of Capoeira

Roger Hudson

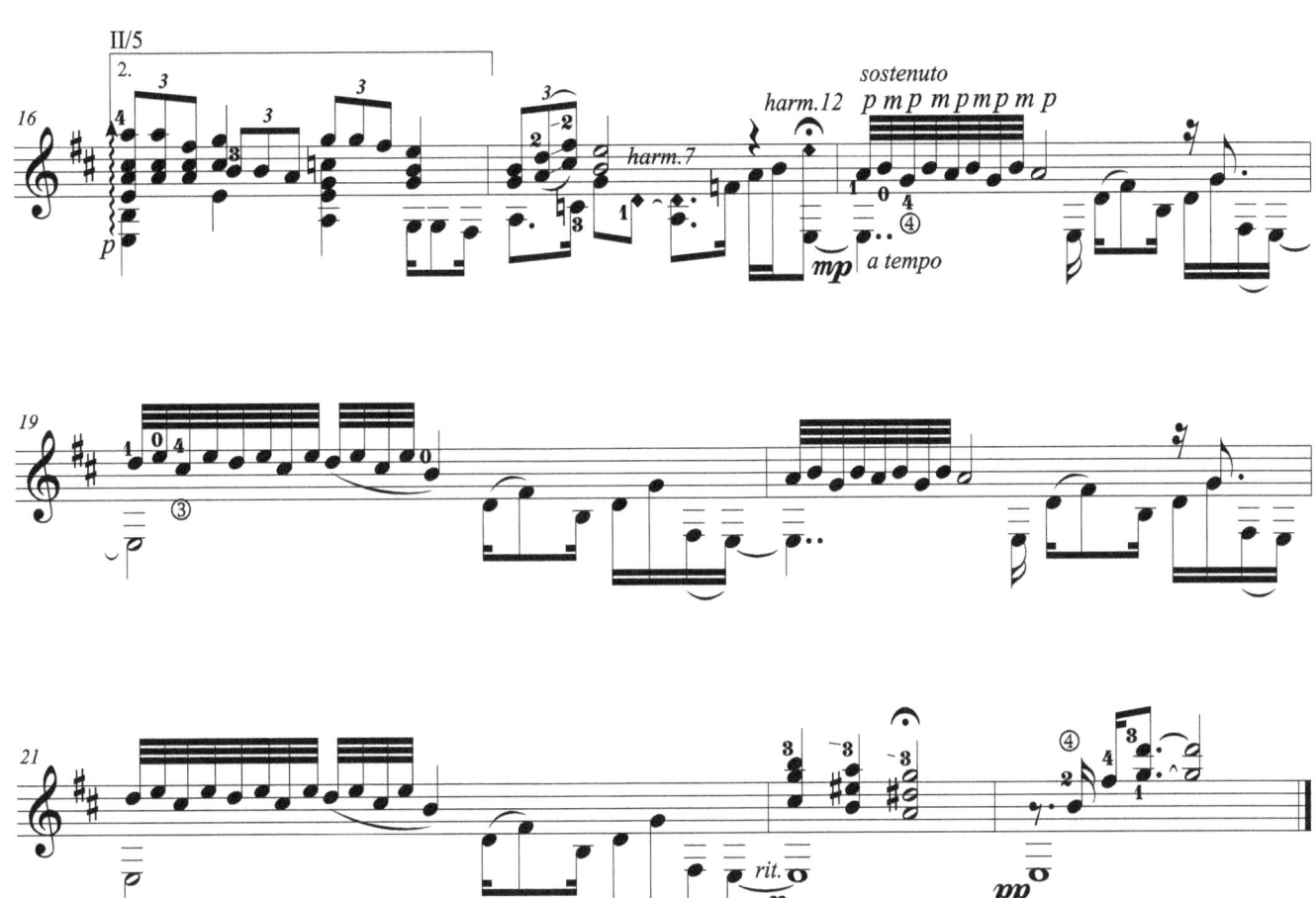

Surreality no. 1

Five Surrealities for Solo Guitar

Roger Hudson

Surreality 2

Five Surrealities for Solo Guitar

Roger Hudson

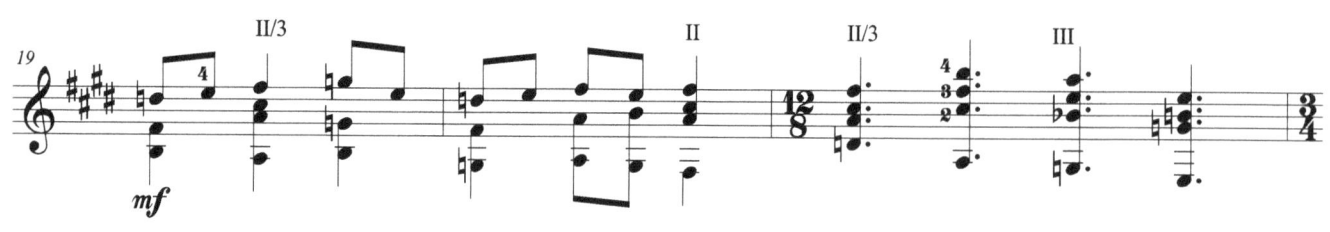

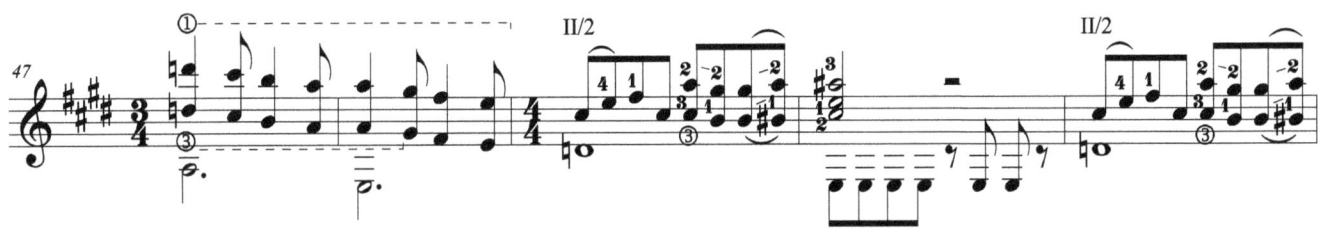

D.C. al Fine
(if desired)

Surreality 3

Five Surrealities for Solo Guitar

Roger Hudson

Surreality 4

Five Surrealities for Solo Guitar

Roger Hudson

Surreality 5
Five Surrealities for Solo Guitar

Roger Hudson

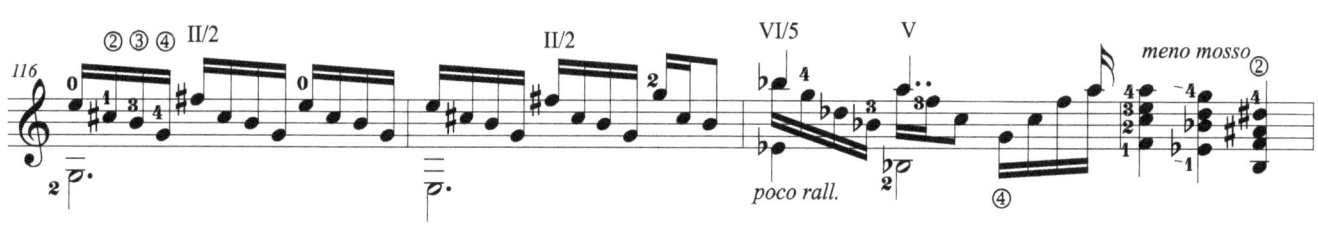

Sweet Surprise

Roger Hudson

Um Puoco de Bossa

(A Little Bit of Bossa)

Roger Hudson

Waiting for a Friend

Roger Hudson

©2018 Roger Hudson ©2020 Roger Hudson Music. All rights reserved. International copyrigfht secured. ASCAP